Editor
Stephanie Buehler, M.P.W., M.A.

Editorial Project Manager
Ina Massler Levin, M.A.

Editor-in-Chief
Sharon Coan, M.S. Ed.

Cover Artist
Sue Fullam

Art Coordinator
Cheri Macoubrie Wilson

Creative Director
Elayne Roberts

Imaging
Ralph Olmedo, Jr.

Product Manager
Phil Garcia

Publisher
Mary D. Smith, M.S. Ed.

How to
Punctuate

Grades 6–8

Author

Michelle Breyer, M.A.

Teacher Created Resources, Inc.
12621 Western Avenue
Garden Grove, CA 92841
www.teachercreated.com
ISBN: 978-1-57690-488-6
©1999 Teacher Created Resources, Inc.
Reprinted, 2016
Made in U.S.A.

Table of Contents

Introduction

About the Book

How to Punctuate is a resource for your classroom. You may use this book as a workbook to teach punctuation or use the individual pages to supplement activities you are already using in your classroom.

The Basics

This book presents punctuation rules that are appropriate for grades 6–8. Pages are organized and titled by groups of rules that apply to various punctuation marks and their usage. A brief description and examples of how to use the rules are given on each page for student reference during practice. Practice exercises are also included to reinforce each concept, and an answer key can be found at the end of the book. It is up to the teacher to select appropriate pages for his or her classroom. For further resources on basic punctuation skills, refer to *How to Punctuate, Grades 3–5*.

Punctuation	Mark
Period	.
Question Mark	?
Exclamation Point	!
Comma	,
Colon	:
Semicolon	;

Assessment

Each section of punctuation instruction is followed by a page that can be used for assessment purposes. The final assessment (p. 43) covers concepts presented throughout the book. All assessments ask students to identify and correct punctuation errors on a line-by-line basis, as well as to correct punctuation errors they find as they copy lines or paragraphs.

Writing Projects

In addition to assessment pages, each section of instruction is followed by a writing project that requires students to apply skills learned in that section. Writing projects include writing a script, writing and addressing a letter, descriptive writing, and writing dialogue. Each writing project may also be used as a form of assessment.

Organization

You may wish students to each create a punctuation reference book made from construction paper and lined notebook paper. In their punctuation books, they could write each of the punctuation rules and examples for easy reference throughout the unit.

Endings Count

There are three different types of punctuation marks that can be used at the end of a sentence.

A **period** is used at the end of a statement or request.	Michael Jordan is a famous basketball player. (statement) Please give me the glue for our project. (request)
A **question mark** is used at the end of a question.	What is the capital of Brazil? Did R. L. Stein write books about ghosts?
An **exclamation point** is used at the end of an exclamation or command.	What a great game! (exclamation) Give me the ball! (command)

Read the paragraph below and add end marks where they are needed.

Have you ever been to a baseball game **?**   My favorite stadium is Dodger Stadium in Los Angeles, California **.**   I love to listen to the sounds of the vendors calling and the crowd cheering **!**   What is your favorite thing to do at a game **?**   Last week, one player hit three home runs **!**   Wow **!**   What an exciting game **!**

Add end marks to the following sentences.

1. The big game is Friday, and we still need to make our uniforms **.**
2. Is Mary going to make the team jerseys, or are we buying them **?**
3. Mary is making them, but what color do you want **?**
4. Blue would be nice, perhaps with white stripes **.**
5. Yes, that would really be great **!**

Write an example of each type of sentence listed below.

1. Statement: _____

2. Question: _____

3. Exclamation: _____

4. Request: _____

5. Command: _____

Abbreviate It

Periods are used after most abbreviations. Use the charts below to help distinguish when punctuation is needed after an abbreviation. If you are not sure whether an abbreviation requires a period, look it up in the dictionary.

Abbreviations Needing Periods	Examples
Personal names	Pearl S. Buck R. L. Stein
Titles used with names	Mr. Mrs. Ms. Sr. Jr. Dr.
States used in a sentence	Calif. Ky. Tenn. S.C. Fla. N.Y.
Addresses	St. Rd. Blvd. P.O. Box
Organizations and companies	Co. Inc. Corp. Ltd. Org.
Times	A.M. P.M. B.C. A.D.

Abbreviations Not Needing Periods	Examples
State names used in addresses	Westminster, CA 92683 Austin, TX 78741
Widely used abbreviations which are all capital letters	CNN PBS UN FBI CIA YMCA VHF PTA NAACP
Many units of metric measurement	cm kg ml mi mg mm

Sometimes there is an abbreviation requiring a period at the end of a sentence. If the sentence would normally end with a period, then a second period is not needed. However, if the sentence ends with a question mark or an exclamation point, then use a period to punctuate the abbreviation and add the correct end mark to the sentence. Here are examples:

Our plane leaves at 8 A.M.   Have you ever been to Rodeo Blvd.?

Read each sentence. Add periods to abbreviations where they are needed.

1. You may fax your order to the Products Dept of the IBM Corp in Orlando, Fla.

2. I know Mr. J P. Sandler is the manager in charge of all orders, but he will not be in until 9:00 AM.

3. Orders by mail should be sent to: Products Dept, IBM Corp, 15962 Sentinel St , P. O. Box 1003, Orlando, FL 32887.

4. Packages weighing less than 5 kg will be sent through the IBM Shipping Dept, but packages weighing over 5 kg will require special handling by UPS.

Use a dictionary to find at least five examples of each type of abbreviation.

Abbreviations with Periods	Abbreviations without Periods
1.	1.
2.	2.
3.	3.
4	4
5.	5.

End Marks and Abbreviations

Assessment:

Rewrite the following sentences, adding end marks where they are needed.

1. Have you ever been to Little Tokyo on the west coast of the USA

   _____

   _____

2. I hear there is a fun place to visit in Los Angeles, California, between First St and Alameda St

   _____

   _____

3. Mr and Mrs Richard P Meyer, Sr , and their son Rich, Jr , plan to take us on our next visit

   _____

   _____

4. We plan on taking the 7:15 PM train from the George T Reynolds Station in Michigan

   _____

   _____

5. Did you know they have compartments with TVs, including cable stations like PBS and CNN

   _____

   _____

6. Our train will arrive at 10:30 AM from Grand Rapids, Michigan, so we will plan to eat lunch near the Sony Corp Bldg in the Japanese Plaza Village

   _____

   _____

7. I can't wait to explore all of the shops on Los Angeles St and Third St with their traditional Japanese cuisine and wares

   _____

   _____

8. Wow What fun it will be to explore another culture

   _____

Writing a Script

Writing Project

A script is commonly used when acting out a play or story. The script describes the actions of the characters and provides the dialogue, or words, the characters speak. There are three main elements to writing a script: the characters, the dialogue, and the stage directions.

The names of the characters should appear at the top of the script as well as in front of the lines each character is to speak. The dialogue is written without quotation marks. Directions for expression, gestures, movement, props, or scenery are written inside parentheses wherever needed.

Read the sample script below. Note how the characters, dialogue, and stage directions are organized. Also pay attention to the different types of end marks and abbreviations. Then follow the directions at the bottom of the page to write your own script.

Characters: **Wilma T. Briggs**   **Samuel L. Johnson**

Narrator: While on a plane headed for New York, Wilma T. Briggs and Samuel L. Johnson strike up a conversation.

Wilma: Tell me, Mr. Johnson, where are you headed in New York? (*Looks at Samuel with a smile, showing interest.*)

Samuel: I'm off to visit relatives who live in New York City, although I didn't think I was ever going to make the 7:00 P.M. flight. I'm on a connection from Dallas, Texas, where I was just finishing a seminar for the Omni Corp. How about you? (*Turns to Wilma and spills a drink in her lap.*)

Wilma: Oh, my goodness! (*Jumps up from seat.*) My new suit from J. C. Penney! My shopping trip in L.A. was a complete waste of time!

Samuel: Please, let me get some help. (*Raises hand to signal help.*) Attendant! Can you get us napkins?

Try It!

1. On a separate sheet of paper, write your own scene between at least two people taking a trip.

2. Include the following punctuation elements in your script:

   End Marks: Give at least one example of each type of sentence: statement, request, question, exclamation, and command.

   Abbreviations: Give at least five different examples of abbreviations.

3. On a second sheet of paper, identify and label the different types of sentences you used in the script. You only need to write one example from your script for each sentence type.

4. On the same paper, identify and label the different types of abbreviations you used in the script. You must identify and label five different types of abbreviations. Staple the two sheets together.

List It

More than two of the same part of speech (except interjections) used in a series are separated by commas to let the reader know where one item in the series ends and the next item begins.

Words in a Series

Hank brought his *bat, ball,* and *glove* to the game on Sunday. (nouns)

At the track meet we will *sprint, hurdle,* and *vault* our way towards a victory. (verbs)

The *violent, steely, crashing* waves menaced the fishermen as they rowed out to sea. (adjectives)

Note: Sometimes the final adjective in a series is closely linked to the noun. In cases like these, do not use a comma before the final adjective.

Example: My brother received a colorful, new *rocking horse* for his birthday. (*not* colorful, new, and rocking horse)

Read the following sentences and add commas where needed.

1. Mrs. Dorsey brought her Persian cat golden retriever and pet goldfish to the veterinarian.
2. The sudden dense fog created a soft gray blanket over the city.
3. If your clothing ever catches on fire, remember to stop drop and roll.
4. As we sped away on the rollercoaster, my stomach jumped bumped and heaved.
5. A bright yellow shining light glowed from the lighthouse to warn travelers at sea.
6. The tutor helped me with my biology algebra and economics homework before finals week.
7. A skillful probing investigator will quickly get to the truth without fail.
8. The novel you are about to read describes the harsh isolated lives of Spartan women in ancient Greece.

Write sentences which use the following parts of speech in a series.

1. Nouns: _____

   _____

2. Verbs: _____

   _____

3. Adjectives: _____

   _____

Commas for Phrases

More than two phrases that are used in a series are separated by commas to let the reader know where one item in the series ends and the next item begins.

Phrases in a Series

Checking the oil pressure, measuring the engine fluids, and *cleaning the windows* was how Randall prepared his vehicle for the long journey through the desert. (participial phrases)

The detectives found fingerprints *on the door, under the sink,* and *in the drawer* when looking for clues. (prepositional phrases)

Raking leaves, mowing grass, and *weeding flower beds* took the entire afternoon. (gerund phrases)

Read each sentence. Underline each of the phrases in the series. Then place commas where needed.

1. We looked in the hall closet under the bed and in the garage for Mother's new umbrella.

2. Anita took care of the birthday party arrangements by calling the caterer blowing up the balloons and hanging the birthday streamers.

3. The rare and beautiful cactus could be found along the canyon gorge in the dried riverbed and atop the plateau.

4. Please stop making so much noise interrupting me and getting into my things while I am on the phone!

5. The video store is around the corner over the bridge and across the street from the bank.

Write a sentence to go with each series of phrases.

1. signing your name, dating the document, and paying the clerk _____

   _____

2. over the fence, through the backyard, and under the house _____

   _____

3. blending the butter, beating the eggs, and adding the flour _____

   _____

Listing Clauses

More than two clauses that are used in a series are separated by commas to let the reader know where one item in the series ends and the next item begins.

Clauses in a Series

We weren't sure *what movie was playing, which theater we would select,* or *when we would leave.* (subordinate clauses)

The table was set, the guests arrived, and *the first course was served* before anyone realized that the host was an imposter. (short independent clauses)

Read each sentence. On the line provided, write only the clauses in a series. Add commas where needed. The first one has been done for you.

1. Dusk came peacefully when the sun lowered the sky grew dark and a golden glow filled the horizon.

   the sun lowered, the sky grew dark, and a golden glow filled the horizon
   _____

2. During the experiment, we examined how much water was needed where the best light source could be obtained and when the seed began to sprout.

   _____

3. It was an exciting moment at the opera when the lights dimmed the curtain rose and the soprano began to sing her aria to the crowd.

   _____

4. The dentist wanted to know how often I brushed my teeth when I flossed and where my last cavity was filled before he would continue with his examination.

   _____

5. When questioned by the teacher, Jeremy told her that Bill drew the picture Maggie wrote the words and Tom put it on the principal's door.

   _____

Create meaningful sentences by finishing each of the following with a series of clauses.

1. As the floodwaters rose, the fireman_____

   _____

2. While on an archaeological dig, the scientists discovered where_____

   _____

Compound It

When a sentence contains more than one subject or more than one predicate, it is called a compound subject or compound predicate. Compound subjects and compound predicates do not require commas unless there are more than two subjects or two predicates. More than two subjects or two predicates used in a sentence are separated by commas.

Compound Subjects

Elizabeth, Todd, and *J. R.* completed the jigsaw puzzle while they were at the cabin.

Either *Mr. Phillip Jones, Mrs. Susan Mackey,* or *Dr. Sullivan* will win the majority of votes.

Among the guest speakers were *an author, an engineer, a CEO,* and *a journalist.*

No comma needed: Either *Alex* or *Bill* will videotape the program for tomorrow's class.

Compound Predicates

We can *go* to the beach, *head* for the mountains, or *stay* right here.

When baking a cake you must *sift* the flour, *measure* the oil, and *beat* the eggs carefully.

The dog *barked, growled,* and *clawed* at the stranger as he tried to enter the house.

No commas needed: The man *was convicted* but later *was found* innocent of the crime.

Read the paragraph containing compound subjects and compound predicates. Add commas where they are needed.

At the end of the spring grading period, our school likes to conduct a class picnic. Mr. Jones Mrs. Read and Ms. Tollison are in charge of the refreshments. On the menu are hot dogs corn on the cob and Ms. Tollison's famous potato salad. Mr. Blevins and Mrs. Ankeny are in charge of decorating the area setting up the tables and getting plenty of trash bags. My favorite part of the picnic is the team games. Last year we ran a three-legged race jumped along in the sack race and tossed eggs to partners. My team won the sack race and egg toss! This year they are adding a ring toss but taking away the sack race. I can't wait for the day to arrive!

Create a sentence with a compound subject and a sentence with a compound verb.

1. Compound subject: _____

   _____

2. Compound predicate: _____

   _____

Punctuating Compound Sentences

A compound sentence contains more than one complete sentence or independent clause. An independent clause has both a subject and a verb. Usually, the independent clauses are joined by connecting words such as *and*, *but*, *or*, *nor*, *for*, *so*, or *yet*. Use a comma before the connecting word when joining independent clauses that make up a compound sentence.

Compound Sentences

As the sun set below the horizon, I felt a cold chill, *and* ominous clouds formed.

I enjoyed watching the game, *but* my father thought it was too long.

During intermission we can buy a soda, or we can wait in our seats and read the program.

Sarah won't give up on her golf lessons, *nor* will she quit trying to beat every player.

Everyone in the audience seemed excited, *for* it was time to begin the circus parade.

We waited over an hour for William to arrive, *so* we finally left without him.

The river looked swift and strong, *yet* the ranger had no trouble navigating the raft.

Combine the two sentences by using a comma and connecting word.

1. We went to a great concert last night. The music was too loud.

   _____

   _____

2. Yadira likes to play soccer during P.E. Her friend Ana likes to play volleyball.

   _____

   _____

3. The fire raged on all through the night. The firemen felt exhausted by the break of day.

   _____

   _____

4. Raymond had trouble sleeping that night. The next day was his graduation day.

   _____

   _____

5. The music in the play was just average. The actors overdramatized their parts.

   _____

   _____

6. Some ants are like high-rise architects. They gather leaves and sew them around twigs to make their nests.

   _____

Commas in a Series or in Compound Sentences

Assessment

Rewrite each of the following sentences, adding commas where needed.

1. The scientist wondered where the insect came from how much it weighed and if it was poisonous.

   _____

   _____

2. While in Washington, D.C., we visited the Jefferson Memorial and the Washington Monument but we never made it to the Capitol.

   _____

   _____

3. The twisting path of the jack rabbit went over the hill between the trees and under a large brown log before disappearing out of sight.

   _____

   _____

4. Before we can set the table, Marie Jeremy or Samantha will unload the plates from the dishwasher.

   _____

   _____

5. He threw the football long hard and fast for he knew it was his team's last chance to make a winning touchdown.

   _____

   _____

6. Jungle travelers must carry a rifle for protection rub insect repellent over their skin and clothes and wear heavy boots to protect their feet.

   _____

   _____

7. Making the bed clearing the dishes from the table and feeding the dog are all my chores yet my younger sister only has to make her bed.

   _____

   _____

8. The male bowerbird builds a strong complex structure for a nest and then he decorates it carefully with bright blue objects to attract a mate.

   _____

   _____

Interrupting Information

Sometimes a writer adds information to a sentence to make it more interesting. This information is in the form of a nonessential phrase or clause. A nonessential phrase or clause adds information that the reader doesn't need in order to understand the basic meaning of the sentence. Therefore, it could be left out without changing the main idea of the sentence. Use commas to set off a nonessential phrase or clause.

Nonessential Phrases and Clauses Need Commas

The sunset, *glowing in the evening dusk,* looked like a ball of fire.

(The sunset looked like a ball of fire.)

Andy Warhol, *who was a famous artist from the 1970s,* created portraits using a silk-screening technique.

(Andy Warhol created portraits using a silk-screening technique.)

Do not set off an essential phrase or clause with commas. An essential phrase or clause cannot be omitted without changing the main idea of the sentence.

Essential Phrases and Clauses Do Not Need Commas

All students *who are carrying beepers or cell phones* must report to the principal's office immediately.

(All students must report to the principal's office immediately. *Which students?*)

The horror movie *that you recommended last week* is not available at the video store.

(The horror movie is not available at the video store. *Which horror movie?*)

Read each sentence. Draw a line under the phrase or clause contained within the sentence. If the phrase or clause is nonessential, set it off with commas.

1. All farmers who are growing the new hybrid of wheat are expected to have a good harvest.

2. Kareem Abdul-Jabbar who holds several NBA records retired from basketball in 1989.

3. Founded in 1636 Harvard College is the oldest college in the United States.

4. The inventions created by Thomas Edison have changed the way people live around the world.

5. Jose had a tremendous fear of spiders which is known as arachnophobia.

6. My blue suit hanging in the closet downstairs looks best with my red and blue tie.

Appositives

An appositive is a noun or pronoun placed beside another noun or pronoun to identify or help explain it. Usually, appositives and appositive phrases are set off by commas. However, if an appositive is needed for meaning or is closely related to the word to which it refers, no commas are needed.

Appositives and Appositive Phrases

Neil Armstrong, the famous American astronaut, was the first person to step on the moon. (commas)

Astronaut Neil Armstrong was the first person to step on the moon. (no commas)

William Brannet, one of the police officers on the scene, apprehended the suspect. (commas)

Police officer William Brannet apprehended the suspect on the scene. (no commas)

Teresa DeAngelis, my cousin, immigrated from France in 1897. (commas)

My cousin Teresa DeAngelis immigrated from France in 1897. (no commas)

Read each set of sentences containing appositives or appositive phrases. Write the letter of the sentence which is punctuated correctly.

1. A. My best friend, Jane is starting her new nursing job tomorrow.

   B. My best friend, Jane, is starting her new nursing job tomorrow.

2. A. They're out of my favorite ice cream, chocolate.

   B. They're out of my favorite chocolate, ice cream.

3. A. The bird watchers spotted a snowy egret, a popular lagoon bird.

   B. The bird watchers spotted a snowy egret a popular, lagoon bird.

4. A. The ship, *Titanic*, sank when it hit a massive iceberg.

   B. The ship, *Titanic* sank when it hit a massive iceberg.

5. A. At Christmas we like to visit my Uncle Alfred who lives in Atlanta.

   B. At Christmas we like to visit my uncle, Alfred, who lives in, Atlanta.

Write three different sentences using appositives or appositive phrases that require commas.

1. _____

_____

2. _____

_____

3. _____

_____

Make a Remark

Use commas to set off words used in direct address or as side remarks or expressions that interrupt the main ideas of sentences. These interrupting remarks are called **parenthetical expressions**.

Direct Address

Amanda, these decorations are for the dance this Friday.

Are you aware, *Joey,* that your library book is due today?

Parenthetical Expressions

The blue dress, however, is my favorite.

The lecture about plant cell mitosis, *I believe,* was too long and boring.

(**Note:** Some parenthetical expressions are not always used as interrupters, and therefore do not need commas.)

In your opinion, what is the best route to take? (interrupting)

I have confidence *in your opinion.* (not interrupting)

The following sentences are each missing a word or expression. Write a word or phrase that makes sense, adding commas where needed.

1. This package is addressed to you _____ and needs to be opened.

2. The president _____ said he hopes to do better next term.

3. _____ I hope you learn to swim this summer.

4. The Bengal tiger _____ is slowly becoming extinct.

5. Do you know _____ when the next train will arrive?

6. I shall invite Rolland _____ to my party on Saturday.

Commonly Used Parenthetical Expressions

after all	generally speaking	nevertheless
at any rate	on the other hand	of course
by the way	I believe	I hope
I suppose	I think	on the contrary
for example	however	for instance
in my opinion	therefore	to say the least

Commas to Set Off Interrupters

Assessment

Read the following paragraph and answer the questions below.

1   Class today we are going to learn about a branch of Buddhism a popular religion
2 practiced in ancient Japan. Buddhism, introduced to Japan by the Chinese and Koreans
3 in the sixth century had a profound effect on the people of Japan. In my opinion the most
4 influential sect or branch was Zen. Zen taught that rigid spiritual and physical discipline
5 would produce an enlightenment of the nature of existence and lead to nirvana a state of
6 everlasting peace. It stressed recognizing the beauty of simplicity and man's
7 harmony within nature. Both meditation and the adherence to defined social rules are
8 components of Zen, and both are believed to keep peace and harmony within society.
9 Throughout the years, Zen ways became absorbed into the lives of all people, regardless
10 of their religious affiliation. This influence can be seen for example in the fine arts,
11 customs, and daily living habits of the people of Japan today.

Select the proper punctuation correction for the following lines of the paragraph and write the appropriate letter on the blank.

Line 1:_____
    A. Add a comma after the words *Class* and *Buddhism.*
    B. Add a comma after the words *Class* and *today.*
    C. No corrections are needed.

Line 3:_____
    A. Add a comma after the word *opinion.*
    B. Add a comma after the words *century* and *opinion.*
    C. No corrections are needed.

Line 4:_____
    A. Add a comma after the word *sect.*
    B. Add a comma after the words *sect* and *rigid.*
    C. No corrections are needed.

Line 5:_____
    A. Add a comma after the word *nirvana.*
    B. Add a comma after the word *produce.*
    C. No corrections are needed.

Line 8:_____
    A. Remove the comma after the word *Zen.*
    B. Add a comma after the word *both.*
    C. No corrections needed.

Line 10:_____
    A. Add a comma after the words *seen* and *example.*
    B. Add a comma after the word *seen.*
    C. No corrections are needed.

Commas

What a Way to Begin

To make a sentence more interesting, a writer will often begin the sentence with an introductory word, phrase, or clause. In these cases, the introductory element should be followed by a **comma**.

Introductory Elements	
Introductory Words	*Yes,* Mary is planning to attend the dance this Friday. *John,* don't you think we should get help before starting?
Introductory Prepositional Phrases	*Beneath the bold and crashing waves,* a lone hermit crab scrambles for his home. *Atop the steep precipice,* the daring mountain climber erected his flag in victory.
Introductory Verbal Phrases	*Judged harshly for her actions,* Jennifer retreated back into the locker room. *To open the door properly,* you must turn the knob while pressing in firmly.
Introductory Adverb Clauses	*When winter finally arrived,* the squirrels had stored over three month's worth of acorns and berries. *Because the total eclipse would last only a few minutes,* Sarah prepared her viewing station in advance.

Read the following sentences containing introductory elements and add commas where needed.

1. Born in 1881 Pablo Picasso was the first male heir on either side of his family.

2. Because the birth was a difficult one Pablo was believed to be stillborn.

3. However his Uncle Salvador did not believe him to be dead and blew a ring of cigar smoke on the infant to elicit a cry.

4. Throughout his long and prosperous career the theme of death in life haunted his imagination and work.

5. Recognized most frequently for his paintings Picasso was also a skilled sculptor, graphic artist, ceramicist, and designer.

6. From 1907 onward his development of cubism abandoned the European Renaissance tradition of art imitating life.

7. Ending with the outbreak of the First World War cubism experienced a highly prosperous period.

8. Why at the height of his career in the early twentieth century Picasso's signature on checks was so valuable that clients refused to cash them.

Adding Introductions

Rearrange each of the sentences below so that it begins with an introductory phrase or clause followed by a comma. The first one has been done for you.

1. We found a large, green caterpillar underneath the hydrangea bush.
   Underneath the hydrangea bush, we found a large, green caterpillar.

2. Marguerite was unable to audition for the school band because she had a sore throat.

3. The temperature increases quickly when the summer sun rises in the desert.

4. We discovered a discarded trunk filled with antique clothes along the side of the road to the old mill.

5. Certain varieties of fish and mollusks thrive on the ocean floor.

6. Michael rode his skateboard to the top of the hill using every ounce of his energy.

7. We must fix the gear shift and replace the timing belt before the car can leave the shop.

8. Rebecca left her library book out on the kitchen table so she wouldn't forget to return it to school.

Bonus: Find two different ways to rearrange the sentences below so that they begin with an introductory phrase or clause.

1. The test pilot soared his mighty jet above the white, billowing clouds to measure its altitude capacity.

   A. _____

   B. _____

2. Jason continued swimming beyond the yellow buoy creating a dangerous situation.

   A. _____

   B. _____

Commas

Conventional Commas

Use **commas** to separate items in certain conventional, or customary, situations.

Dates	The Towne Book Fair begins on Monday, September 25. Our Constitution was signed on September 17, 1787.
Addresses	The Kentucky Derby is held each spring in Louisville, Kentucky. The address you requested is 453 Bear St., Chicago, IL 69697.
Friendly Letter **Salutation and Closing**	Dear Grandma Martha, Sincerely yours,

Read the following letter and envelope. Insert commas where needed.

Tuesday March 16 1999

Dear Aunt Judy

    I want to thank you for the lovely new dress you sent to me for my birthday. I'm sorry you were unable to attend my party on Saturday March 13. We had lots of fun. I plan to come visit you in Lynchburg Virginia this summer. Mother wants you to check your calendar for July. She has booked me on a flight to arrive Wednesday July 27 in the evening. Please write or call to let us know if that date is all right. I can't wait to see you!

Yours truly
Kara

Kara James
7008 Milton Road
Los Angeles CA 90049

        Mrs. Judy Kimball
        1454 Dresser Road
        Lynchburg Virginia 20546

Commas

Assessment

Read the following paragraphs, adding commas where needed.

Did I ever tell you about the time our dishwasher which usually works fine turned into a foaming mess? It was on Saturday December 3 that our parents left for the boat show in Del Mar. Teresa and I were left to do the dishes a chore we both detest. After battling our way through piles of filthy plates bowls and glasses I headed upstairs to watch television. Teresa unfortunately was left to run the dishwasher. Being the younger and less experienced sister Teresa overestimated the amount of soap to use. After about twenty minutes I heard a shrill loud cry for help. When I heard her alarmed tone of voice I knew there was something desperately wrong. I ran downstairs to find the dishwasher floor and much of Teresa covered in a thick foamy flow of bubbles. Quickly I made my way across the slippery floor fought through the bubbles and turned off the machine.

Now of course we were left to clean up the disaster created by my incompetent younger sibling for we didn't want Mom and Dad to see it when they got home. Getting the mop and sponge we began to work diligently at the task. We were satisfied with our effort after nearly an hour of steady work. We then put everything away crossed our fingers and tried turning the newly cleaned dishwasher back on. To our noticeable relief the washing cycle began without a hitch. We waited for further impending doom but everything seemed normal. Deciding to keep the incident a secret we both continued on with our regularly scheduled activities.

Our parents returned home and both thanked us for cleaning the kitchen so well. I couldn't help but feel a bit guilty when they went on an on about how responsible trustworthy and dependable we were; however I still couldn't bring myself to tell them the truth. We were each given a hug and a raise in our allowance. Should we have taken the praise and money? So what would you do if this ever happened to you?

Friendly Letter

Writing Project

Practice the many different ways to use the comma by completing the following writing project. Refer to work earlier in this unit (pages 8–20) for specific examples.

1. On a separate sheet of paper, write a letter to a friend about a recent adventure. Make sure you have at least one example for each category on the chart below.

2. Address an envelope to your friend and include a return address.

3. Fill in the chart below, using items from your letter and envelope.

4. Turn in the completed letter, envelope, and chart.

Uses of the Comma	Examples from Letter or Envelope
Use commas to separate items in a series— single words, phrases, and clauses.	
Use a comma and a conjunction to join two independent clauses and create a compound sentence.	
Use commas to set off expressions that interrupt sentences.	
Use commas after certain introductory elements.	
Use commas to separate dates and addresses.	
Use a comma after the opening and closing of a letter.	

22

Basic Semicolons

A **semicolon** looks and acts like a period and comma combined. It separates complete independent clauses like a period, while also separating items within a sentence like a comma. Use a semicolon instead of a period only when the ideas in the independent clauses are closely related.

I called Jessica. She will arrive in thirty minutes.	(two independent clauses separated by a period)
I called Jessica, and she will arrive in thirty minutes.	(compound sentence using a comma and a conjunction—and, but, or, for, yet)
I called Jessica; she will arrive in thirty minutes.	(two independent clauses joined by a semicolon)

Note: Don't use too many semicolons. When editing your work, decide if it is better to make a compound sentence with a comma and a conjunction, two complete sentences, or a sentence with several commas rather than use a semicolon.

Grammatically Correct: In the deserts of northern Africa, the sun beats down all day practically every day of the year; the plants there, some of which are found nowhere else in the world, are tough, thick, and drought resistant.

Better: In the deserts of northern Africa, the sun beats down all day, practically every day of the year. The plants there, some of which are found nowhere else in the world, are tough, thick, and drought resistant.

Read the following sentences and add semicolons where needed.

1. On our first trip to California, I wanted to visit the San Diego Zoo my little sister wanted to go to Disneyland.
2. Our parents settled the dispute for us they decided we could go to both places.
3. At the zoo we saw a zebra, elephant, and lion the tigers were not in their display area.
4. Three days later we went to Disneyland it has imaginative rides.
5. We can't wait to vacation in California again there are so many sights to see.

Choose two sentences from above to rewrite as compound sentences joined by conjunctions and commas.

1. _____

_____

2. _____

_____

Semicolons with Transitions

A conjunctive adverb or a transitional expression is used to show the relationship between two independent clauses joined by a semicolon.

Commonly Used Conjunctive Adverbs and Transitional Phrases

accordingly	of course	in spite of	for instance	otherwise
besides	furthermore	in other words	in conclusion	consequently
therefore	however	instead	on the other	that is
as a result	moreover	meanwhile	hand	in fact
in addition	for example	indeed	nevertheless	after all

★★

Almost all areas on earth have been explored by modern scientists. They have now begun research on the floors of the sea.

(two independent clauses separated by a period)

Almost all areas on earth have been explored by modern scientists; as a result, they have now begun research on the floors of the sea.

(two independent clauses joined by a semicolon with a transitional expression followed by a comma)

Write the following sentences using a semicolon, an appropriate conjunctive adverb or transitional phrase, and a comma.

1. Jonathan Filianga decided not to go to the movies. He went to the mall with some friends.

   _____

   _____

2. Algebra was Anthony's most difficult subject in school. He studied for it more than he studied for any other subject.

   _____

   _____

3. Many words in the English language come from our Native American population. The words raccoon, canoe, and toboggan are all Native American words.

   _____

   _____

4. Some people prefer a wet climate. Others prefer living where it is dry.

   _____

   _____

5. Mr. Billings, our principal, announced the students who passed the physical fitness test. He passed out medals to each winner.

   _____

   _____

Too Many Commas

A **semicolon** rather than a comma and conjunction may be needed to join independent clauses to form a compound sentence, particularly if there are commas already within the independent clauses.

> A short, stocky man entered the dark, smoky lounge; his tall, rough partner followed closely behind.
>
> We will read chapter one on Monday, chapter two on Wednesday, and chapter three on Friday; and over the weekend I want you to review the vocabulary for all three chapters.

Read each of the following independent clauses. Create another independent clause to follow, and join it to the first one with a semicolon and a conjunction. The first one has been done as an example.

1. The thick, heavy cloud of smoke billowed through the broken upstairs window;

   and the firefighter's orange coat could be seen flashing through the haze.

2. A gallant, gray horse galloped and leaped through the tall, green grass

   _____

   _____

3. After you do the dishes, I want you to clean the floor, empty the trash, and clean your room

   _____

   _____

4. Annie, my friend from New York, came to visit the museum, park, and beach

   _____

   _____

5. Today the sun shone brightly against the massive, azure waves and soft, golden sand

   _____

   _____

6. Skateboarding down the steep, slick hill, Martin ducked and curled like a wiry, slim surfer

   _____

   _____

Colons

Colons are used in conventional situations more often than in text. Below are a few cases.

Time	Ratios	Bible Verses	Business Letter Salutations
3:15 P.M.	2 to 1	John 3:16	Dear Sir:
4:17 A.M.	2:1	Genesis 1:7	To Whom It May Concern:

The most common placement for **colons** in text is before a list of items. If using a **colon** before your list, do not place it directly after a verb or a preposition. A **colon** is most often used with expressions like *as follows* or *the following*.

Correct	On our camping trip we will need to bring sleeping bags, a camping stove, a flashlight, warm clothes, and a week's supply of food.
Incorrect	On our camping trip we will need to bring: sleeping bags, a camping stove, a flashlight, warm clothes, and a week's supply of food.
Correct	On our camping trip we will need to bring the following items: sleeping bags, camping stove, a flashlight, warm clothes, and a week's supply of food.
Correct	This recipe is made from chicken, curry, onions, brown sugar, and sour cream.
Incorrect	This recipe is made from: chicken, curry, onions, brown sugar, and sour cream.
Correct	This recipe includes these ingredients: chicken, curry, onions, brown sugar, and sour cream.

Read each list of items. Write a sentence with a colon inserted before each list.

1. bait, tackle, net, and hooks _____

_____

2. ham sandwich, grapes, string cheese, orange juice, and a chocolate chip cookie _____

_____

3. protractor, compass, calculator, ruler, and pencils _____

_____

4. basketball, tennis, swimming, and bowling_____

_____

Semicolons and Colons

Assessment

Write the letter of the correctly punctuated sentence on the blank.

_____ 1. A. Raising your own vegetables can be fun, fulfilling, and economical; but for the experience to be all three, you will need to invest some time in planning.

B. Raising your own vegetables can be fun, fulfilling, and economical, but for the experience to be all three, you will need to invest some time, in planning.

_____ 2. A. Before you take a shovel to the soil, you need to research. your planting season, climate zone, and soil conditions.

B. Before you take a shovel to the soil, research the following variables: your planting season, climate zone, and soil conditions.

_____ 3. A. Plan to grow vegetables that will thrive under your conditions; in addition, consider what vegetables you really like, and choose from these.

B. Plan to grow vegetables that will thrive under your conditions, in addition; consider what vegetables you really like, and choose from these.

_____ 4. A. You should also know, how many people you plan to feed; it is all too easy to overplant, and then work too hard, to maintain a garden with more vegetables, than you can use.

B. You should also know how many people you plan to feed; it is all too easy to overplant, and then work too hard to maintain a garden with more vegetables than you can use.

_____ 5. A. As soon as you know which vegetables you're going to plant; you're ready to prepare the garden.

B. As soon as you know which vegetables you're going to plant, you're ready to prepare the garden.

_____ 6. A. Work the soil, adding organic matter 2:1 with existing dirt, for example, two scoops of organic mulch for every one scoop of garden dirt.

B. Work the soil, adding organic matter 2,1 with existing dirt; for example two scoops of organic mulch, for every one scoop of garden dirt.

_____ 7. A. You usually have two options when planting vegetables: planting seeds or setting out young plants bought at a nursery.

B. You usually have two options when planting vegetables; planting seeds or setting out young plants bought at a nursery.

Descriptive Writing

Writing Project

Practice the many uses of the **comma**, **semicolon**, and **colon** while writing a descriptive poem. Make sure you have at least one correct example of each punctuation mark within your poem.

1. Think of a scene in nature that elicits sights, sounds, smells, textures, and feelings. It could be from anywhere on earth and during any season.

2. Use the chart below to brainstorm your thoughts about this scene. Remember, you are not telling a story with actions and events. Try only to describe the scene with your different senses.

Sights: _____

Sounds: _____

Textures: _____

Smells: _____

Feelings: _____

3. Using a separate sheet of paper, begin writing complex phrases and sentences for each of your items on the list. Use a thesaurus to help increase your vocabulary and add interest to your sentences.

4. Organize your sentences to achieve a natural flow and rhythm to the poem. You may want to organize the sentences by the different senses or by the different areas of the scene you are describing.

5. Check again to make sure you have at least one correct example of a **comma, semicolon,** and **colon** in your poem. Below is an example of a poem.

As I dive carelessly into the cool blue sea, the smooth, sultry seaweed meanders softly around my wet feet. Each nimble branch reaches up to the crystal sky, anticipating a sip of fresh sea air; it wraps around my legs, playfully tugging and pulling at my free limbs.

The soft, rippling water echoes of dancing porpoises singing their songs of joy like mermaids with high-pitched voices. Gulls soar into the air, squawk to join the chorus, and dip and dive over the splashing waves; their music is in rhythm with each bountiful plunge.

I emerge from this beautiful sapphire abyss with three memories: the salty water tingling along my face like the flow of a cool silk scarf, the sandy floor squishing between my toes, and the exhilaration of floating weightlessly in this vast azure cove.

Which Is Which?

Sometimes it is difficult to choose between **italics** (or **underlining**) or **quotation marks** when you are referring to a title or name in your writing. Use the chart below to help distinguish which type of punctuation is appropriate.

Italics or Underlining

Type of Title	Examples		
Books	*The Golden Goblet*	*The Outsiders*	*The Master Puppeteer*
Plays	*Phantom of the Opera*	*Romeo and Juliet*	*Death of a Salesman*
Periodicals	*The New York Times*	*National Geographic*	*Newsweek*
Works of Art	*The Thinker*	*Mona Lisa*	*The Last Supper*
Films	*Star Wars*	*Schindler's List*	*Lion King*
Television Programs	*7th Heaven*	*Full House*	*Wall Street Week*
Full-length LPs/CDs	*Unforgettable*	*No Fences*	*Man of Steel*
Long Musical Compositions	*Don Giovanni*	*A Sea Symphony*	*Peter and the Wolf*
Ships	*Titanic*	USS *Nimitz*	*Queen Mary*
Aircraft	*Spirit of St. Louis*	*Air Force One*	*Spruce Goose*
Spacecraft	*Apollo 12*	*Voyager 1*	USS *Enterprise*

Note: When reading printed material or using a computer to compose your writing, the title should appear in italics. Since it is not practical to handwrite in italics, underlining can be substituted when italics are not an available option.

Quotation Marks
Used to Refer to a Smaller Section of Work
Found Within a Larger Body of Work

Type of Title	Examples	
Short Stories	"The Tell-Tale Heart"	"The Rule of Names"
Poems	"Mother to Son"	"The Road Not Taken"
Articles	"Free Speech and Free Air"	"Marriage in the '90s"
Songs	"America the Beautiful"	"Stairway to Heaven"
Television Episodes	"Heart of a Champion"	"The Trouble with Tribbles"
Chapters and Other Book Parts	"Expanding West"	"English: Origins and Uses"

Note: Ask yourself if the title of a work appears inside a larger body of work. If so, the title belongs inside quotation marks. If the title is for a longer body of work that stands alone, it should be underlined or typed in italics.

© Teacher Created Resources, Inc.   29   #2488 How to Punctuate

Which Is Which? *(cont.)*

Use the charts on page 29 to help you punctuate the following titles correctly.

1. Uncle Dan reads The Wall Street Journal each morning before leaving for work.

2. I have seen The Secret Garden, a movie adapted from Frances H. Burnett's novel, three times.

3. O. Henry wrote a funny short story called The Ransom of Red Chief.

4. My little brother loves for me to sing Man in the Moon before he sleeps each night.

5. Jeremy got a job on the Indian Princess, a cruise ship to Mexico, for the summer.

6. In Dudley Randall's poem Ancestors, he asks thought-provoking questions.

7. The newsstand was out of this month's issues of Sports Illustrated and Good Housekeeping.

8. The final act will be a medley of songs from George Gershwin's opera Porgy and Bess.

Follow the directions to write complete sentences containing titles. Be creative in your compositions. An example has been provided.

Example: Name a ship and an aircraft. Last year our family visited Long Beach, where we toured the <u>Queen Mary</u> and <u>Spruce Goose</u>.

1. Name a song and an album._____

   _____

2. Name a television program. Create a title for an episode. _____

   _____

3. Name a magazine. Create a title for an article that could be found in this magazine. _____

   _____

4. Name a movie and an actor from the movie. _____

   _____

5. Name a book that contains short stories or poems, and then name the title of a story or poem.

   _____

6. Create the name of a musical play and tell the name of a song from that play. _____

   _____

Adding Emphasis

Occasionally, writers will use **italics** (or **underlining**) to express an emphasis in their statement. This is usually done to help clarify the meaning of the sentence rather than to show emotion. Read each of the sentences below that emphasize words in italics. Notice how the meaning of the sentence changes, depending on which word is emphasized.

Is *Samantha* the new student in Mrs. Jones' English class? (Is it Samantha or someone else?)

Is Samantha the *new* student in Mrs. Jones' English class? (Is she new or not?)

Is Samantha the new *student* in Mrs. Jones' English class? (Is she a student or an aide?)

Is Samantha the new student in *Mrs. Jones'* English class? (Is she with another teacher?)

Is Samantha the new student in Mrs. Jones' *English* class? (Isn't she in her other class?)

A. Underline the appropriate word or set of words to convey the emphasis described.

1. Are you looking at the directions on page 48? (Are you looking at the right page?)

2. Are you looking at the directions on page 48? (Are you reading the right information?)

3. Are you looking at the directions on page 48? (Are you actually reading, or is the book just open?)

A writer will also use **underlining** or **italics** to refer to words, letters, or figures within a sentence.

What is the difference between the words *concave* and *convex?*

Don't forget to drop the *y* before you add *ied.*

B. Read the following sentences. If the sentence is correct, write C. If the sentence is incorrect, write the sentence correctly.

1. Sometimes I add an extra gh to the word throughout, and it comes out <u>throughought</u>.

   _____

2. Janine finally found her division mistake; the *45* was in the wrong column.

   _____

3. The teacher reminded the class to drop the e before adding -ing to a word.

   _____

4. I sometimes mix up the meanings of <u>effect</u> and affect.

   _____

Underlining or Italics and Quotation Marks

Assessment

Write the letter of the correctly punctuated sentence.

_____ 1. A. Are you certain that he's the *new* delivery boy?
                B. Are you certain <u>that</u> he's the new delivery boy?
                C. Are you certain that he's the "new" delivery boy?

_____ 2. A. Picasso's painting "Guernica" is named after a Spanish town destroyed in war.
                B. Picasso's painting *Guernica* is named after a Spanish town destroyed in war.
                C. Picasso's painting Guernica is named after <u>a Spanish town</u> destroyed in war.

_____ 3. A. "Be Our Guest" is a popular song from the Disney movie *Beauty and the Beast*.
                B. *Be Our Guest* is a popular song from the *Disney movie* "Beauty and the Beast".
                C. "Be Our Guest" is a popular song from the Disney movie "Beauty and the Beast".

_____ 4. A. Please listen to the sounds the ch and sh make before reading each word.
                B. Please listen to the sounds the "ch and sh" make before reading each word.
                C. Please listen to the sounds the *ch* and *sh* make before reading each word.

_____ 5. A. My father reads the *Washington Post* for its articles on "local politics".
                B. My father reads the <u>Washington Post</u> for its articles on local politics.
                C. My father reads the "Washington Post" for its articles on local politics.

_____ 6. A. They say the band aboard <u>Titanic</u> played the hymn <u>Nearer My God to Thee</u> as the ship sank.
                B. They say the band aboard *Titanic* played the hymn "Nearer My God to Thee" as the ship sank.
                C. They say the band aboard Titanic played the hymn <u>Nearer My God to Thee</u> as the ship sank.

_____ 7. A. Please refer to the map on "page 28."
                B. Please refer to *the* map on page 28.
                C. Please refer to the *map* on page 28.

_____ 8. A. Open your book to "Chapter 5: Exploration in the New Land" on page 345.
                B. Open your book to Chapter 5: <u>Exploration in the New Land</u> on page 345.
                C. Open your <u>book</u> to "Chapter 5: Exploration in the New Land" on page 345.

_____ 9. A. Did you read *All About Teething* in last month's issue of *Parenting Magazine*?
                B. Did you read "All About Teething" in last month's issue of <u>Parenting Magazine</u>?
                C. Did you read "All About Teething" in last month's issue of Parenting Magazine?

_____ 10. A. Only capitalize and underline the word *the* when it is part of the book title.
                B. Only capitalize and underline the word the when it is part of the <u>book title</u>.
                C. Only capitalize and underline the word <u>the</u> when it is part of the book *title*.

Quote This

Use **quotation marks** to enclose a person's exact words when speaking. This is called a *direct quotation.*

"I am going to the store in fifteen minutes," Sara called down the hall.

Mrs. Barnes told the class, **"Write your name in the upper right-hand corner."**

(**Note:** Do not use quotation marks around an **indirect quotation** or a rewording of a direct quotation.)

Direct Quotation: "Are you going to the dance Friday?" asked Maria.
Indirect Quotation: Maria asked if I was going to the dance on Friday.

Direct Quotation: Derek shouted, "You are a poor loser!" and turned to go home.
Indirect Quotation: Derek shouted that I was a poor loser before he went home.

Read each of the following sentences. Add quotation marks around the direct quotations where needed.

1. Kaya asked, What do you think Sara's message means?

2. Are you all right? the fireman called to the boy stuck down in the well.

3. My mother said that she wanted to go to the movies tonight.

4. This dress is too tight, Sara remarked as she prepared to meet her friends.

5. Molly asked what I thought of her collection of prehistoric fossils.

6. Suddenly a loud shriek filled the air, Help! It's getting me!

7. What are some of the characteristics of a plant cell? Mr. Bross asked his class.

8. I am certain that I know what I'm doing, explained Mitchell as he turned the crank.

9. Brian wasn't able to explain what he was doing with the money when his parents questioned him.

10. Looking over the back seat, Mayra requested, Please move your head so I can see to back up.

Punctuating and Capitalizing Quotes

A direct quotation always begins with a capital letter regardless of where the quotation appears in the sentence. However, punctuating direct quotations varies, depending on their placement.

Speaker Before: When the name of the person doing the speaking comes before the direct quote, the direct quote is preceded by a comma. The quote is punctuated like a regular sentence and enclosed by quotation marks.

> Ann said, *"I hope you find what you are looking for."*
> Mrs. Paul asked, *"Do you know the capital of Peru?"*
> Tamara exclaimed, *"Let me go!"*

Speaker After: When the name of the person doing the speaking comes after the direct quote, the punctuation is varied. If the direct quote is a question or exclamation, then the ending punctuation should be added. If, however, the sentence is a statement or request, then a comma is used in place of a period. In all cases, a period is placed at the end of the entire sentence.

> *"I hope you find what you are looking for,"* said Ann.
> *"Do you know the capital of Peru?"* asked Mrs. Paul.
> *"Let me go!"* exclaimed Tamara.

Write the following sentences, adding punctuation marks where needed. Capitalize the first word of the direct quote.

1. Michael shouted let's get busy with the paint

2. Those who deny freedom to others deserve it not for themselves stated Abraham Lincoln

3. Has anyone in this group ever climbed Mount Everest asked the mountain guide

4. Mr. Cummings said please watch your step through the pond

5. Donna and Chandra complained we don't want to do the dishes

6. Help cried the frightened girl as she grasped the end of the rope

7. What is the time difference between New York and Los Angeles he asked the flight attendant

Speaker in Between

To add interest to a passage with many direct quotations, such as a passage containing dialogue between characters, a writer may choose to vary the placement of the speaker's name. The speaker's name can come *before* the direct quotation, *after* the direct quotation, or *in between* the direct quotation.

Speaker in Between: When the name of the speaker comes in between (or interrupts) the direct quotation, the second part of the quotation begins with a lowercase letter. Commas are used to separate the quote from the rest of the sentence.

"What are some of the animals," asked Mr. Petok, *"that scientists discovered in the Amazon rain forest?"*

"Finish the dishes and complete your homework," said Mother firmly, turning to look me in the eyes, *"before you even think of watching television."*

Read each direct quote. Create an appropriate speaker for each quote and place the name or description of the speaker in the location identified. Punctuate the sentence properly, using the information presented on pages 34 and 35. The first one has been done for you.

1. The Egyptian form of heaven was known as the Field of Reeds. (speaker in between)

   "The Egyptian form of heaven," said the museum curator, "was known as the Field of Reeds."

2. Don't throw that ball in here! (speaker before)

   _____

3. Have you ever been on a roller coaster? (speaker after)

   _____

4. Emperor Qin had over 4,000 statues of soldiers buried in his tomb. (speaker in between)

   _____

5. Plant cell mitosis is a rather simple yet mystifying process. (speaker in between)

   _____

6. Do you know if Charlie is coming with us? (speaker before)

   _____

7. Please hide me from the sheriff! (speaker after)

   _____

8. Are you certain that he is the new president? (speaker in between)

   _____

Direct Quotations

Assessment

Revise the following paragraphs by adding commas, end marks, and quotation marks where necessary. Capitalize any words that begin a direct quotation.

Jeremy, do you ever think about maps Hannah asked

only when I'm lost or taking a trip Jeremy replied

well said Hannah let me tell you some of the things I learned about maps in my geography class

sure Jeremy said I love trivia

Hannah began Ptolemy was a great mapmaker and geographer. He lived from A.D. 90–168 during the reign of the Roman Empire. Ptolemy gathered information from travelers and traders to compose a remarkably accurate map of the ancient world. However, things changed with the fall of the Roman Empire

why, what happened Jeremy asked

for the next 1,000 years maps became distorted. Ptolemy's work was forgotten and maps were formed around important landmarks. For example Hannah continued Christian mapmakers often placed Jerusalem in the center of their maps with the East at the top.

when was a more accurate world map produced Jeremy asked. I mean, at some point they must have discovered what really existed to the north, south, east, and west Jeremy replied Didn't explorers set the record straight

why, yes Hannah remarked in the early 1400s, scholars found copies of Ptolemy's work, and this stimulated a new interest in exploration and world geography. As new places were discovered, maps were charted and changed to reflect a change in the way people viewed the world

Thanks, Hannah said Jeremy for the interesting information. I'll think of Ptolemy the next time I'm lost and need a good map

More Underlining or Italics and Quotation Marks

Assessment

Each of the following sentences require italics (or underlining), quotation marks, or both. Write the letter which states the correction needed.

_____ 1. The best chapter in our history book is the last one, European Enlightenment.

    A. Change to *European Enlightenment.*

    B. Change to "European Enlightenment."

    C. Change to <u>European Enlightenment</u>.

_____ 2. "I answered all twenty questions, replied Fletcher, but I don't think they're all correct."

    A. Place quotation marks after *questions.*

    B. Change to <u>twenty questions</u>.

    C. Place quotation marks after *questions* and before *but.*

_____ 3. Gone With the Wind was much more exciting when seen in the movie theater than it was on our television set in class.

    A. Change to *Gone With the Wind.*

    B. Change to "Gone With the Wind."

    C. Place quotation marks around *Gone With the Wind* and *television set.*

_____ 4. Play the Michael Jackson CD again, James, Leticia called from her room.

    A. Place quotation marks before *Play* and after *James.*

    B. Place quotation marks before *Play* and after *again.*

    C. Place quotation marks before *Play* and after *room.*

_____ 5. Lydia wrote an article called School Food or School Fraud? for our local newspaper, the North County Times.

    A. Change to "School Food or School Fraud?" and "North County Times."

    B. Change to "School Food or School Fraud?" and <u>North County Times</u>.

    C. Change to *School Food or School Fraud?* and *North County Times.*

_____ 6. "Can I read Old Yeller for my book report? asked Erica.

    A. Change to <u>Old Yeller</u> and add quotation marks after *report?*

    B. Place quotation marks around Old Yeller and after *report?*

    C. Change to <u>Old Yeller</u> and place quotation marks after *Erica.*

Writing Dialogue

Writing Project

Below is a script for a scene from a play. Change the format so that it reads like a passage in a book with dialogue.

1. Begin the passage with some information to set up the scene. Close the dialogue with a conclusion to the scene.

2. Remember to begin a new paragraph (indent) each time you change speakers.

3. Vary your quotation technique so that some quotes have the speaker before, speaker after, or speaker in between. (See pages 33–36.)

4. Do not change the words the characters are speaking. However, do add information to describe the characters' actions and feelings. This will make the passage more interesting.

5. Use a thesaurus to find different words with similar meanings as *said* so that you can use a variety of terms in your dialogue.

6. Have a friend help you edit your rough draft. Then write or type your final draft to share with the class. Note all of the different ways this scene can be interpreted as a dialogue.

(The scene opens at Claire's house. A school dance is Friday, and Claire is picking out what she wants to wear. The doorbell rings, and Claire answers it.)

Claire: Hello, Christopher. What are you doing here?

Christopher: Hi, Claire. I came over to see if you are going to the dance on Friday.

Claire: Yes, Amanda, Elizabeth, and I are planning on going together. Why?

Christopher: Oh, well, I guess you wouldn't want to go with me, then.

Claire: Christopher, are you asking me to the dance?

Christopher: Kind of, but I didn't realize that you already had plans.

Claire: Plans can always be changed. I'm sure my friends could manage without me.

Christopher: Does that mean you want to go with me?

Claire: Yes, Chris, it does.

Christopher: Good. I'll meet you in front of the entrance at 7:00 and we can go in together.

Claire: Okay. I'll meet you there. I'm glad you asked me.

Christopher: Me, too.

Showing Possession

Using **apostrophes** to show possession is often confusing for students. Yet, there are only a few basic rules.

To form a possessive for a singular noun add an apostrophe and an *s*.

the student**'s** records   Mrs. Smith**'s** red car   the dress**'s** collar

Exception: Sometimes a proper name ending in *s* would be too difficult to pronounce with an added apostrophe and an *s*. Therefore, you must use your judgment.

Mr. Jones**'** backyard   Hercules**'** victories   Los Angeles**'** population

To form the possessive for a plural noun, add an apostrophe.

ball players**'** team   citizens**'** vote   many flowers**'** stems

Exception: If the plural does not end in an *s*, add both the apostrophe and an *s*.

mice**'s** cheese   women**'s** locker room   children**'s** books

Common mistakes: You do not use an apostrophe to make a noun plural. You do not use an apostrophe with possessive personal pronouns like the following: *yours, ours, theirs, its, hers,* or *his.*

Show possession in the following examples. Check to see if the noun is singular or plural before adding an apostrophe and an *s*. The first one has been done for you.

1. the food belonging to our dog   <u>our dog's food</u>

2. careers belonging to women   _____

3. comments made by my friend   _____

4. some toys that belong to my baby   _____

5. the horn that is attached to it   _____

6. tickets that belong to the passengers   _____

7. some clothes for the children   _____

8. a store owned by Chris   _____

9. a paintbrush belonging to an artist   _____

10. invitations sent by the hostess   _____

Contraction Action

A contraction is a shortened form of a word or group of words. An **apostrophe** is used to signify where letters or numerals have been left out.

Common Contractions

I am...I'm	1995...'95	let us...let's
they had...they'd	of the clock...o'clock	she would...she'd
you have...you've	he is...he's	are not...aren't
should not...shouldn't	will not...won't	does not...doesn't

Do not, however, confuse contractions with possessive pronouns.

Contractions

It's raining outside. (It is)
It's been a long winter. (It has)
Who's next for popcorn? (Who is)
Who's been helping you? (Who has)
There's only one exit. (There is)
There's been a change in our plans. (There has)
They're going to Florida. (They are)
You're a great teacher. (You are)

Possessive Pronouns

Its muffler is broken.

Whose idea was it to use black?

The extra change is **theirs**.

Their house is in Miami.
Your school work has improved.

Copy the following paragraph, creating contractions wherever possible. (Note: In formal writing, one should limit the number of contractions one uses.)

Last week my brother decided to pay us a visit. He has been meaning to fly out from Georgia for the past year, but he has not had the opportunity yet. I am very excited to see him, for he has not been to our home since last August. My mom and dad can not wait to hear about his new job. They have been talking to him on the phone, but it is not the same as speaking to him in person. He will fly by airplane and arrive on Saturday. It is a five-hour flight from Georgia, and we must not miss it!

The last time I saw my brother, he had just finished college. We were all very proud of him. He applied for a job in the computer industry and immediately got hired. That is why he has been living in Georgia. We have missed him, but we are proud of the work he has accomplished. I am sure he will not want to hang out at the same places we did when we were in high school together. Now, there are other things he likes to do. It will be interesting to see him again, and we will look forward to picking him up at the airport on Saturday.

Hyphens

Hyphens aren't used very frequently, but you will find them in some compound words and numbers.

Compound Words	Compound Names	Compound Numbers/Fractions
brother-in-law	Jackie Joyner-Kersee	sixty-five
G-rated	Daniel Day-Lewis	four-tenths

Hyphens are also used to divide a word at the end of a line. When using hyphens in this way, follow these rules:

1. Divide a word only between syllables.
2. Do not divide a one-syllable word.
3. Divide a word containing a hyphen at the hyphen.
4. Do not divide a word so that one letter stands alone.
5. Whenever possible, write the entire word on the next line instead of dividing it.

Write the following expressions, inserting hyphens as needed.

1. thirty five balloons _____

2. the city of Wilkes Barre _____

3. one half cup of sugar _____

4. six hundred fifty six dollars and ninety five cents _____

5. Rolando Hinojosa Smith _____

6. Forty second Street _____

7. the state of Schleswig Holstein _____

Write each sentence so that one word is divided at the end of the line properly.

1. Some word-processing programs will automatically divide a word at the end of a line and insert a hyphen.

   _____

   _____

2. Such a division will sometimes break one of the rules above, so be sure to check your printout carefully.

   _____

   _____

Apostrophes and Hyphens

Assessment

Each of the following sentences contains at least one mistake in the use of apostrophes or hyphens. Write each sentence correctly.

1. Half of Melodys allowance goes into her savings account.

   _____

2. The girl's didnt say when theyd be back.

   _____

3. Twenty five student council member's votes are needed to change the schools' song.

   _____

4. If your going to the base-ball game, remember to take a-long your mothers blanket.

   _____

5. Jesses' dream is to have fif-teen palomino horses.

   _____

6. Lets find out when the next game is play'ed.

   _____

7. Everybodys favorite tour stop in Virginia was Mount Vernon, George Washingtons home.

   _____

8. Dont' you remember they're story about catching twenty six butterflie's?

   _____

9. The recipe called for two third's of a cup of milk and one half tablespoon of butter.

   _____

10. Mrs. Vincents son owe's Frank three hundred forty seven dollars and sixty eight cents.

   _____

Unit Assessment

Punctuate each of the following sentences correctly.

1. The worlds fastest typist Cortez Peters has won thirteen international contests and he can type two hundred fifty words per minute

2. Ted Julias father reads the Wall Street Journal every morning while he drinks his coffee

3. Sheilas Aunt Mary made a delicious salad with the following vegetables from our garden lettuce tomatoes and carrots

4. Fill out both sides of the form said the Drivers Training clerk

5. When Dr. Sloan ran after a taxicab his pants became soiled from a muddy puddle

6. Marias first pet which she got when she turned ten was a cat she named it Fluffy

7. Rubin come in and sit down commanded Mr Fester our history professor

8. How many times have you seen The Secret Garden a movie adapted from Frances H Burnetts novel

9. The soft subtle dyes used in the Navajo womans rug are made from natural ingredients

10. Wasnt President John F Kennedy shot on November 22 1963 in Dallas Texas

11. Please dont sing Ive Been Working on the Railroad anymore because its making me crazy

12. The cats mewed and the dogs barked however the chickens remained silent throughout the night

Unit Assessment *(cont.)*

13. Wow Thats the longest home run Darrels ever hit

14. Brian asked Mom will you take us to football practice

15. After the rain stopped the sparrows and robins searched the wet slippery ground for worms.

16. Well I do know that my flight arrives at 8 15 PM and I had better be prepared for the meeting

17. I read in the Encyclopedia Britannica that Thomas Jefferson loved Italian food and he even ordered pasta from Italy

18. Everybody had told her in fact that she couldnt succeed if she didnt try

19. In one of the barns stalls we found an old pitch fork some rusty cans and musty dirty hay

20. Jerry Spinelli a Newbery Award winner wrote the book Maniac Magee said Joseph

21. Did you see the highlights from the St Patricks Day Parade on CNNs six o clock broadcast

22. Beverly my cousin lives at 7008 Floral Terrace Carlsbad Ca 92009

23. To get a better view of the sunset Jim and I rode our bikes to the top of Sutters Hill

24. Did you read the article called A Short Sprint about the life and death of Florence Griffith Joyner

25. Wont you stay pleaded Kathy The bands about to begin and I want to dance

Answer Key

Page 4

Have you ever been to a baseball game? My favorite stadium is Dodger Stadium in Los Angeles, California. I love to listen to the sounds of the vendors calling and the crowd cheering. What is your favorite thing to do at a game? Last week one player hit three home runs. Wow! What an exciting game!

1. The big game is Friday, and we still need to make our uniforms.
2. Is Mary going to make team jerseys, or are we buying them?
3. Mary is making them, but what color do you want?
4. Blue would be nice, perhaps with white stripes.
5. Yes, that would really be great!

Page 5

1. You may fax your order to the Products Dept. of the IBM Corp. in Orlando, Fla.
2. I know Mr. J. P. Sandler is the manager in charge of all orders, but he will not be in until 9:00 A.M.
3. Orders by mail should be sent to: Products Dept., IBM Corp., 15962 Sentinel St., P.O. Box 1003, Orlando, FL 32887.
4. Packages weighing less than 5 kg will be sent through the IBM Shipping Dept., but packages weighing over 5 kg will require special handling by UPS.

Page 6

1. Have you ever been to Little Tokyo on the west coast of the U.S.A.?
2. I hear it is a fun place to visit in Los Angeles, California, between First St. and Alameda St.
3. Mr. and Mrs. Richard P. Meyer, Sr., and their son Rich, Jr., plan to take us on our next visit.
4. We plan to take the 7:15 P.M. train from the George T. Reynolds Station in Michigan.
5. Did you know they have compartments with TVs, including cable stations like PBS and CNN?
6. Our train will arrive at 10:30 A.M. from Grand Rapids, Michigan, so we will plan to eat lunch near the Sony Corp. Bldg. in the Japanese Plaza Village.
7. I can't wait to explore all of the shops on Los Angeles St. and Third St. with their traditional Japanese cuisine and wares.
8. Wow! What fun it will be to explore another culture!

Page 8

1. Mrs. Dorsey brought her Persian cat, golden retriever, and pet goldfish to the veterinarian.
2. The sudden dense fog created a soft, gray blanket over the city.
3. If your clothing ever catches on fire, remember to stop, drop, and roll.
4. As we sped away on the rollercoaster, my stomach jumped, bumped, and heaved.
5. A bright, yellow, shining light glowed from the lighthouse to warn travelers at sea.
6. The tutor helped me with my biology, algebra, and economics homework before finals week.
7. A skillful, probing investigator will quickly get to the truth without fail.
8. The novel you are about to read describes the harsh, isolated lives of Spartan women in ancient Greece.

Page 9

1. We looked in the hall closet, under the bed, and in the garage for Mother's new umbrella.
2. Anita took care of the birthday party arrangements by calling the caterer, blowing up the balloons, and hanging the birthday streamers.
3. The rare and beautiful cactus could be found along the canyon gorge, in the dried riverbed, and atop the plateau.
4. Please stop making so much noise, interrupting me, and getting into my things while I am on the phone!
5. The video store is around the corner, over the bridge, and across the street from the bank.

Page 10

2. how much water was needed, where the best light source could be obtained, and when the seed began to sprout.
3. the lights dimmed, the curtain rose, and the soprano began to sing her aria to the crowd.
4. how often I brushed my teeth, when I flossed, and where my last cavity was filled
5. Bill drew the picture, Maggie wrote the words, and Tom put it on the principal's door.

Page 11

At the end of the spring grading period, our school likes to conduct a class picnic. Mr. Jones, Mrs. Read, and Ms. Tollison are in charge of the refreshments. On the menu are hot dogs, corn on the cob, and Ms. Tollison's famous potato salad. Mr. Blevins and Mrs. Ankeny are in charge of decorating the area, setting up the tables, and getting plenty of trash bags. My favorite part of the picnic is the team games. Last year we ran a three-legged race, jumped along in the sack race, and tossed eggs to partners. My team won the sack race and egg toss! This year they are adding a ring toss but taking away the sack race. I can't wait for the day to arrive!

Page 12

1. We went to a great concert last night, but [yet] the music was too loud.
2. Yadira likes to play soccer during P.E., but [yet, and] her friend Ana likes to play volleyball.
3. The fire raged on all through the night, so [therefore, consequently] the firemen felt exhausted by the break of day.
4. Raymond had trouble sleeping that night, for [as, because] the next day was his graduation day.
5. The music in the play was just average, and the actors overdramatized their parts.
6. Some ants are like high-rise architects, for they gather leaves and sew them around twigs to make their nests.

Page 13

1. The scientist wondered where the insect came from, how much it weighed, and if it was poisonous.
2. While in Washington, D.C., we visited the Jefferson Memorial and the Washington Monument, but we never made it to the Capitol.
3. The twisting path of the jack rabbit went over the hill, between the trees, and under a large, brown log before disappearing out of sight.
4. Before we can set the table, Marie, Jeremy, or Samantha will unload the plates from the dishwasher.
5. He threw the football long, hard, and fast, for he knew it was his team's last chance to make a winning touchdown.

Answer Key *(cont.)*

6. Jungle travelers must carry a rifle for protection, rub insect repellent over their skin and clothes, and wear heavy boots to protect their feet.

7. Making the bed, clearing the dishes from the table, and feeding the dog are all my chores, yet my younger sister only has to make her bed.

8. The male bowerbird builds a strong, complex structure for a nest, and then he decorates it carefully with bright, blue objects to attract a mate.

Page 14

1. All farmers <u>who are growing the new hybrid of wheat</u> are expected to have a good harvest.

2. Kareem Abdul-Jabbar, <u>who holds several NBA records,</u> retired from basketball in 1989.

3. <u>Founded in 1636,</u> Harvard College is the oldest college in the United States.

4. The inventions <u>created by Thomas Edison</u> have changed the way people live around the world.

5. Jose had a tremendous fear of spiders, <u>which is known as arachnophobia.</u>

6. My blue suit, <u>hanging in the closet downstairs,</u> looks best with my red and blue tie.

Page 15

1. B
2. A
3. A
4. B
5. A

Page 17

Line 1: A
Line 3: B
Line 4: C
Line 5: A
Line 8: C
Line 10: A

Page 18

1. Born in 1881, Pablo Picasso was the first male heir on either side of his family.

2. Because the birth was a difficult one, Pablo was believed to be stillborn.

3. However, his Uncle Salvador did not believe him to be dead and blew a ring of cigar smoke on the infant to elicit a cry.

4. Throughout his long and prosperous career, the theme of death in life haunted his imagination and work.

5. Recognized most frequently for his paintings, Picasso was also a skilled sculptor, graphic artist, ceramicist, and designer.

6. From 1907 onward, his development of cubism abandoned the European Renaissance tradition of art imitating life.

7. Ending with the outbreak of the First World War, cubism experienced a highly prosperous period.

8. Why, at the height of his career in the early twentieth century, Picasso's signature on checks was so valuable that clients refused to cash them.

Page 19

2. Because she had a sore throat, Marguerite was unable to audition for the school band.

3. When the summer sun rises in the desert, the temperature increases quickly.

4. Along the side of the road to the old mill, we discovered a discarded trunk filled with antique clothes.

5. On the ocean floor, certain varieties of fish and mollusks thrive.

6. Using every ounce of his energy, Michael rode his skateboard to the top of the hill.

7. Before the car can leave the shop, we must fix the gear shift and replace the timing belt.

8. So she wouldn't forget to return it to school, Rebecca left her library book out on the kitchen table.

Bonus

1. To measure its altitude capacity, the test pilot soared his mighty jet above the white, billowing clouds.

   Above the white, billowing clouds, the test pilot soared his mighty jet to measure its altitude capacity.

2. Beyond the yellow buoy, Jason continued swimming, creating a dangerous situation.

   Creating a dangerous situation, Jason continued swimming beyond the yellow buoy.

Page 20

Tuesday, March 16, 1999

Dear Aunt Judy,

I want to thank you for the lovely new dress you sent to me for my birthday. I'm sorry you were unable to attend my party on Saturday, March 13. We had lots of fun. I plan to come visit you in Lynchburg, Virginia, this summer. Mother wants you to check your calendar for July. She has booked me on a flight to arrive Wednesday, July 27, in the evening. Please write or call to let us know if that date is all right. I can't wait to see you!

Yours truly,

Kara

Kara James
7008 Milton Road
Los Angeles, CA 90049

Mrs. Judy Kimball
1454 Dresser Road
Lynchburg, Virginia 20546

Page 21

Did I ever tell you about the time our dishwasher, which usually works fine, turned into a foaming mess? It was on Saturday, December 3, that our parents left for the boat show in Del Mar. Teresa and I were left to do the dishes, a chore we both detest. After battling our way through piles of filthy plates, bowls, and glasses, I headed upstairs to watch television. Teresa, unfortunately, was left to run the dishwasher. Being the younger and less experienced sister, Teresa overestimated the amount of soap to use. After about twenty minutes, I heard a shrill, loud cry for help. When I heard her alarmed tone of voice, I knew there was something desperately wrong. I ran downstairs to find the dishwasher, floor, and much of Teresa covered in a thick, foamy flow of bubbles. Quickly, I made my way across the slippery floor, fought through the bubbles, and turned off the machine.

Now, of course, we were left to clean up the disaster created by my incompetent younger sibling, for we didn't want Mom and Dad to see it when they got home. Getting the mop and sponge, we began to work diligently at the task. We were satisfied with our effort after nearly an hour of steady work. We then put everything away, crossed our fingers, and tried turning the newly cleaned dishwasher back on. To our noticeable relief, the

Answer Key *(cont.)*

washing cycle began without a hitch. We waited for further impending doom, but everything seemed normal. Deciding to keep the incident a secret, we both continued on with our regularly scheduled activities.

Our parents returned home, and both thanked us for cleaning the kitchen so well. I couldn't help but feel a bit guilty when they went on and on about how responsible, trustworthy, and dependable we were; however, I still couldn't bring myself to tell them the truth. We were each given a hug and a raise in our allowance. Should we have taken the praise and money? So, what would you do if it ever happened to you?

Page 23

1. On our first trip to California, I wanted to visit the San Diego Zoo; my little sister wanted to go to Disneyland.
2. Our parents settled the dispute for us; they decided we could go to both places.
3. At the zoo we saw a zebra, elephant, and lion; the tigers were not in their display area.
4. Three days later we went to Disneyland; it has imaginative rides.
5. We can't wait to vacation in California again; there are so many sights to see.

Page 27

1. A
2. B
3. A
4. B
5. B
6. A
7. A

Page 30

(**Note:** Underlining may be substituted for italics.)

1. *The Wall Street Journal*
2. *The Secret Garden*
3. "The Ransom of Red Chief"
4. "Man in the Moon"
5. *Indian Princess*
6. "Ancestors"
7. *Sports Illustrated, Good Housekeeping*
8. *Porgy and Bess*

Page 31

A.1. *48*
2. *directions*
3. *looking*
B.1. Sometimes I add an extra *gh* to the word *throughout*, and it comes out throughought.
2. C
3. The teacher reminded the class to drop the *e* before adding *-ing* to a word.
4. I sometimes mix up the meanings of *effect* and *affect*.

Page 32

1. A
2. B
3. A
4. C
5. B
6. B
7. C

8. A
9. B
10. A

Page 33

1. Kaya asked, "What do you think Sara's message means?"
2. "Are you all right?" the fireman called to the boy stuck down in the well.
3. No corrections
4. "This dress is too tight," Sara remarked as she prepared to meet her friends.
5. No corrections
6. Suddenly a loud shriek filled the air, "Help! It's getting me!"
7. "What are some of the characteristics of a plant cell?" Mr. Bross asked his class.
8. "I am certain that I know what I'm doing," explained Mitchell as he turned the crank.
9. No corrections
10. Looking over the back seat, Mayra requested, "Please move your head so I can see to back up."

Page 34

1. Michael shouted, "Let's get busy with the paint!"
2. "Those who deny freedom to others deserve it not for themselves," stated Abraham Lincoln.
3. "Has anyone in this group ever climbed Mount Everest?" asked the mountain guide.
4. Mr. Cummings said, "Please watch your step through the pond."
5. Donna and Chandra complained, "We don't want to do the dishes."
6. "Help!" cried the frightened girl as she grasped the end of the rope.
7. "What is the time difference between New York and Los Angeles?" he asked the flight attendant.

Page 35

Answers will vary.

Page 36

"Jeremy, do you ever think about maps?" Hannah asked.

"Only when I'm lost or taking a trip," Jeremy replied.

"Well," said Hannah, "let me tell you some of the things I learned about maps in my geography class."

"Sure," Jeremy said. "I love trivia."

Hannah began, "Ptolemy was a great mapmaker and geographer. He lived from A.D. 90–168 during the reign of the Roman Empire. Ptolemy gathered information from travelers and traders to compose a remarkably accurate map of the ancient world. However, things change with the fall of the Roman Empire."

"Why, what happened?" Jeremy asked.

"For the next 1,000 years maps became distorted. Ptolemy's work was forgotten, and maps were formed around important landmarks. For example," Hannah continued, "Christian mapmakers often placed Jerusalem in the center of their maps, with the East at the top."

"When was a more accurate world map produced?" Jeremy asked. "I mean, at some point they must have discovered what really existed to the north, south, east, and west," Jeremy replied. "Didn't explorers set the record straight?"

"Why, yes!" Hannah remarked. "In the early 1400s, scholars found copies of Ptolemy's work, and this stimulated a new interest in exploration and world geography. As new places were discovered, maps were charted and changed to reflect a change in the way people viewed the world."

"Thanks, Hannah," said Jeremy, "for the interesting information. I'll think of Ptolemy the next time I'm lost and need a good map."

Page 37
1. B
2. C
3. A
4. A
5. B
6. A

Page 39
2. women's careers
3. my friend's comments
4. my baby's toys
5. its horn
6. the passengers' tickets
7. the children's clothes
8. Chris' store or Chris's store
9. an artist's paintbrush
10. the hostess's invitations

Page 40
Last week my brother decided to pay us a visit. He's been meaning to fly out from Georgia for the past year, but he hasn't had the opportunity yet. I'm very excited to see him, for he hasn't been to our home since last August. My mom and dad can't wait to hear about his new job. They've been talking to him on the phone, but it isn't the same as speaking to him in person. He'll fly by airplane and arrive on Saturday. It's a five-hour flight from Georgia, and we mustn't miss it!

The last time I saw my brother, he'd just finished college. We were all very proud of him. He applied for a job in the computer industry and immediately got hired. That's why he's been living in Georgia. We've missed him, but we're proud of the work he's accomplished. I'm sure he won't want to hang out at the same places we did when we were in high school together. Now, there're other things he likes to do. It'll be interesting to see him again, and we'll look forward to picking him up at the airport on Saturday.

Page 41
1. thirty-five balloons
2. the city of Wilkes-Barre
3. one-half cup of sugar
4. six hundred fifty-six dollars and ninety-five cents
5. Rolando Hinojosa-Smith
6. Forty-second Street
7. the state of Schleswig-Holstein

Page 42
1. Half of Melody's allowance goes into her savings account.
2. The girls didn't say when they'd be back.
3. Twenty-five student council members' votes are needed to change the school's song.
4. If you're going to the baseball game, remember to take along your mother's blanket.
5. Jesse's dream is to have fifteen palomino horses.
6. Let's find out when the next game is played.
7. Everybody's favorite tour stop in Virginia was Mount Vernon, George Washington's home.
8. Don't you remember their story about catching twenty-six butterflies?
9. The recipe called for two-thirds of a cup of milk and one-half tablespoon of butter.
10. Mrs. Vincent's son owes Frank three hundred forty-seven dollars and sixty-eight cents.

Pages 43–44
1. The world's fastest typist, Cortez Peters, has won thirteen international contests, and he can type two hundred fifty words per minute.
2. Ted, Julia's father, reads the *Wall Street Journal* every morning while he drinks his coffee.
3. Sheila's Aunt Mary made a delicious salad with the following vegetables from our garden: lettuce, tomatoes, and carrots.
4. "Fill out both sides of the form," said the Drivers' Training clerk.
5. When Dr. Sloan ran after a taxicab, his pants became soiled from a muddy puddle.
6. Maria's first pet, which she got when she turned ten, was a cat; she named it Fluffy.
7. "Rubin, come in and sit down!" commanded Mr. Fester, our history professor.
8. How many times have you seen *The Secret Garden*, a movie adapted from Frances H. Burnett's novel?
9. The soft, subtle dyes used in the Navajo woman's rug are made from natural ingredients.
10. Wasn't President John F. Kennedy shot on November 22, 1963, in Dallas, Texas?
11. Please don't sing "I've Been Working on the Railroad" anymore, because it's making me crazy.
12. The cats mewed and the dogs barked; however, the chickens remained silent throughout the night.
13. Wow! That's the longest home run Darrel's ever hit.
14. Brian asked Mom, "Will you take us to football practice?"
15. After the rain stopped, the sparrows and robins searched the wet, slippery ground for worms.
16. Well, I do know that my flight arrives at 8:15 P.M., and I had better be prepared for the meeting.
17. I read in the *Encyclopedia Britannica* that Thomas Jefferson loved Italian food, and he even ordered pasta from Italy.
18. Everybody had told her, in fact, that she couldn't succeed if she didn't try.
19. In one of the barn's stalls we found an old pitchfork; some rusty cans; and musty, dirty hay.
20. "Jerry Spinelli, a Newbery Award winner, wrote the book *Maniac Magee*," said Joseph.
21. Did you see the highlights from the St. Patrick's Day Parade on the CNN's six o' clock broadcast?
22. Beverly, my cousin, lives at 7008 Floral Terrace, Carlsbad, CA 92009.
23. To get a better view of the sunset, Jim and I rode our bikes to the top of Sutter's Hill.
24. Did you read "A Short Sprint," the article about the life and death of Florence Griffith-Joyner?
25. "Won't you stay?" pleaded Kathy. "The band's about to begin and I want to dance."

Made in the USA
Middletown, DE
08 September 2020